Share your artwork with us on Instagram @JobsWithJess

Disclaimer. The information provided in this book is for educational and informational purposes only. The author and the publisher disclaim liability for any loss or damage suffered by any person as a result of the information in this book. Any action you take upon the information in this book is at your own risk. The accuracy and completeness of the information provided herein, and the opinions stated herein are not guaranteed or warranted to produce any particular results, and the advice and strategies contained herein are not suitable for every individual. Neither the publisher nor the author is engaged in rendering professional service. If other expert assistance is required, the services of a competent professional should be sought. Neither the publisher nor the author shall be liable for any loss or loss of profit or any other commercial damages, including but not limited to special, incidental, consequential, or other damages.

Copyright © 2021 JM Career Enterprises LLC

All Rights Reserved. No part of this book may be reproduced or used in any manner without the prior written permission of the copyright owner, except for the use of brief quotations in a book review.

Paperback ISBN: 978-1-7367363-0-2

OPPORTUNITIES

FUTURE

MONEY

My income **INCREASES** every year

I DESERVE TO BE PAID FOR MY TIME

www.ingramcontent.com/pod-product-compliance
Lightning Source LLC
Chambersburg PA
CBHW081422080526
44589CB00016B/2637